THE PLACE: THE LIBRARY OF COMIC BOOK BIOGRAPHIES. THE MISSION: CREATE THE GRAPHIC BIOGRAPHY OF SPEAKER OF THE HOUSE NANCY PELOSI.

★★★ WE HAVE TO DECIDE ON *SOMETHING*. THIS IS A *BIG* RESPONSIBILITY.

THEY ALREADY HAVE BIOGRAPHIES OF PALIN AND CLINTON. WE HAVE TO GET THIS THING *RIGHT.*

THE LIBRARY OF COMIC BOOK SUPERHERO TALES.

★★★ BUT WE CAN'T EVEN START IT. WE NEED A MORE NEUTRAL BEGINNING, SOMETHING MORE FACT-BASED.

LIBRARY OF UNREALISTICALLY ENDOWED COMIC BOOK SUPERHEROINES. HOME TO THE "RED SONJA WHAT IS THAT ARMOR BIKINI ACTUALLY PROTECTING SPECIAL RESEARCH WING."

★★★ SHE'S JUST *SO* POLARIZING, YOU KNOW.

★★★ SEEMS YOU EITHER LOVE HER OR HATE HER.

★★★ HOW DO YOU WRITE A FAIR BIOGRAPHY WITH THAT?

★★★ WHY DON'T WE START SIMPLE, THEN? WITH HER INSPIRATION.

★★★ AH, YOU MEAN HER FATHER, TOMMY D'ALESANDRO.

★★★ TOMMY THE ELDER.

FIRST ELECTED TO THE MARYLAND HOUSE OF DELEGATES IN 1926, D'ALESANDRO WAS THE MOST IMPORTANT POLITICAL LEADER IN BALTIMORE IN THE 1920S AND 1930S.

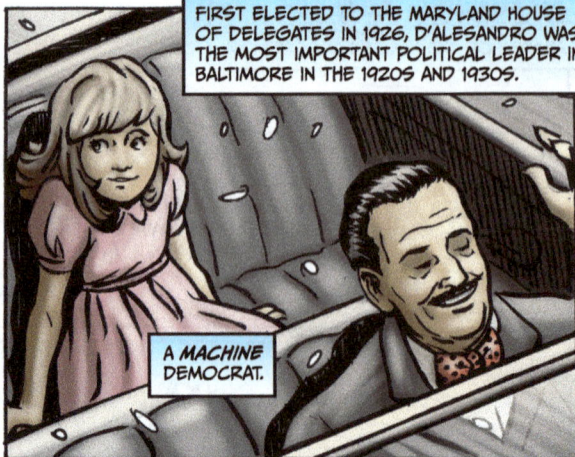

A *MACHINE* DEMOCRAT.

TOMMY D'ALESANDRO LOVED TO CAMPAIGN. HE WAS ALWAYS RUNNING FOR SOMETHING. AND USUALLY WINNING. HE SAID THE ONLY TIME HE DIDN'T WIN WAS WHEN HE FORGOT TO WEAR HIS LUCKY BOW TIE.

AND HIS DAUGHTER, NANCY, SHE *LOVED* IT ALL, TOO, DIDN'T SHE?

TOMMY NOTCHED FIVE STRAIGHT TERMS AS A U.S. CONGRESSMAN. THAT'S FIVE STRAIGHT ELECTION VICTORIES. *AMAZING.*

AND *THEN* HE WENT ON TO SERVE AS MAYOR OF BALTIMORE FOR THREE TERMS. HE EVEN HAD TIME TO HAVE *SIX* CHILDREN.

NANCY *LOVED* IT ALL.

★ ★ TOMMY FOR MAYOR AGAIN!

THAT'S *PERFECT.* NANCY PELOSI, A *CAREER* POLITICIAN.

ACTUALLY, *NO.* NANCY WENT TO TRINITY COLLEGE IN WASHINGTON D.C., WHERE SHE STUDIED POLITICAL SCIENCE. IT'S WHERE SHE MET PAUL PELOSI.

IT WAS A *STORYBOOK* ROMANCE.

I THINK I JUST THREW UP IN MY MOUTH.

THEY WERE MARRIED IN 1963.

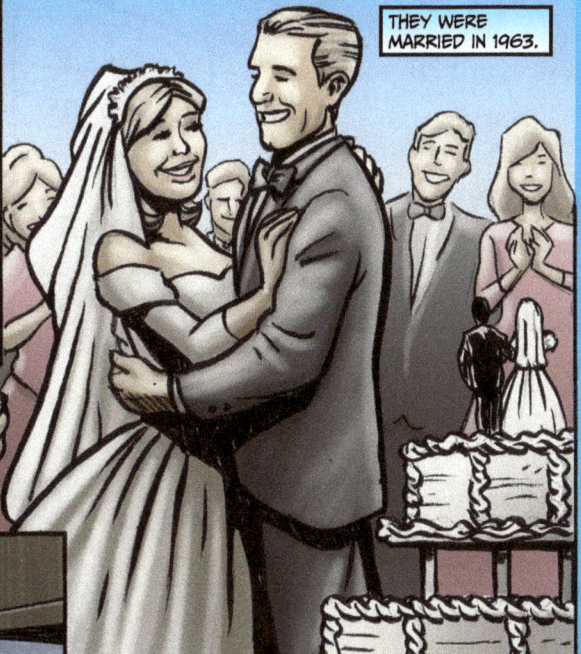

THEY'VE BEEN TOGETHER EVER SINCE. THEY HAVE FIVE CHILDREN, FOUR GIRLS AND ONE BOY.

TWO *COMMIES* WHO FOUND EACH OTHER, NO DOUBT. HOW SWEET.

THEY'VE BEEN MARRIED FOR 46 YEARS. NOT LIKE MOST OF YOUR "FAMILY-VALUES" REPUBLICANS. LIKE YOUR BUDDY NEWT, WHO ASKED HIS FIRST WIFE TO SIGN DIVORCE PAPERS WHILE SHE WAS IN THE HOSPITAL *RECOVERING FROM CANCER SURGERY.*

YOU MISERABLE *&&*!

AND THEN, HE ASKED HIS *SECOND* WIFE – WHOM HE WAS HAVING AN AFFAIR WITH WHEN HIS FIRST WIFE WAS GOING THROUGH ALL THOSE CANCER SURGERIES – FOR A DIVORCE BY PHONING HER ON *MOTHER'S DAY!*

TURNS OUT, NEWT HAD BEEN HAVING AN AFFAIR WITH HIS FORMER CONGRESSIONAL AIDE. HE MARRIED HER, EVEN THOUGH SHE WAS YOUNG ENOUGH TO BE HIS DAUGHTER.

AND LET'S NOT EVEN MENTION LARRY CRAIG. THAT MAN MUST HAVE THE *WIDEST* STANCE IN THE UNIVERSE!

ANYWAY, MAYBE WE SHOULD GO THE TRADITIONAL BIOGRAPHY ROUTE. CHRONOLOGICAL.

THAT MAY BE THE *SAFEST* ROUTE TO GO.

LET'S SKIP TO 1969, THEN. THE PELOSI FAMILY MOVED TO SAN FRANCISCO, PAUL PELOSI'S HOMETOWN.

YES, THE LIBERAL NUTS FLOCK TO THE *HOME BASE* FOR LIBERAL NUTTINESS.

ANTI-AMERICAN, THAT PLACE IS. THEY SELL THE MOST *FLAMMABLE* FLAGS THERE. WE SHOULD JUST CUT SAN FRANCISCO OFF OF THE COUNTRY. GET A BIG BUZZ SAW AND SLICE THE CITY OFF, LET IT FALL INTO THE SEA.

YOU GUYS ALWAYS HAVE SUCH A BURR UP YOUR BUTT ABOUT SAN FRANCISCO. I HAVE MY THEORIES ABOUT *THAT.*

NOT INTERESTED.

ANYWAY, NANCY WASN'T EXACTLY THE FLAMING LIBERAL YOU LIKE TO PAINT HER AS. SHE DID SOME VOLUNTEER WORK FOR THE LOCAL DEMOCRATIC PARTY, BUT SHE MOSTLY CONCENTRATED ON RAISING HER KIDS.

OH, THOSE KIDS. YOU KNOW THAT HER DAUGHTER, ALEXANDRA, MADE THAT FILM SLAMMING GEORGE BUSH.

YES, HE'S SO HARD TO SLAM.

SHE CALLED IT *JOURNEYS WITH GEORGE.*

YEP. SHE HAD THE EXTREME PLEASURE OF FOLLOWING GEORGE BUSH AROUND THE CAMPAIGN TRAIL IN 2000.

BRUSH CLEARING DIGEST

ZZZZZ...

CAN'T EXPECT A *BALANCED* DOCUMENTARY FROM A PELOSI.

WHO WANTS AN EXCLUSIVE NOW... ANYONE? ANYONE?

ME! ME! TALK TO ME!

PRESS

ACTUALLY, IT WASN'T A BUSH SLAM AT ALL. IF ANYTHING, SHE RIPS ON THE MEDIA FOR THE WAY THEY LAP UP WHATEVER PRESIDENTIAL CANDIDATES TELL THEM.

LOOKS LIKE WIDE BRIM IS IN THIS YEAR...

THE FILM EARNED SIX EMMY NOMINATIONS.

AH, THE EMMY. THE AWARD FOR MOVIES NOT GOOD ENOUGH TO ACTUALLY MAKE IT INTO MOVIE THEATERS.

ALEXANDRA ISN'T THE ONLY PELOSI DOING WELL FOR HERSELF, EITHER. THE PELOSI CHILDREN ARE A GIFTED LOT.

ALL GOOD CARD-CARRYING LIBERALS, I'M SURE.

PAUL PELOSI JR. IS AN ENVIRONMENTALIST AND POPULAR SPEAKER ON ENVIRONMENTAL TOPICS.

SURE, JUST WHAT WE NEED, MORE ENVIRONMENTALISTS.

CAMPAIGN BOOT CAMP
BASIC TRAINING FOR FUTURE LEADERS

CHRISTINE PELOSI

Book Signing Today, Christine Pelosi!

U.S. HOUSE OR BUST!

U.S. HOUSE OR BUST!

AND CHRISTINE PELOSI WROTE HER OWN BOOK, CAMPAIGN BOOT CAMP: BASIC TRAINING FOR FUTURE LEADERS.

CAN'T WAIT TO SEE THE MOVIE!

U.S. HOUSE OF REPRESENTATIVES

ENOUGH WITH THE HALLMARK MOMENTS, HUH? LET'S GET INTO THE MEAT.

WHEN ARE WE GOING TO TALK ABOUT HOW MUCH NANCY PELOSI HATES AMERICA?

CHRISTINE ALSO DIRECTS A BOOT CAMP THAT PREPARES DEMOCRATS FOR CONGRESSIONAL CAMPAIGNS. SHE'S CREDITED WITH HELPING 23 DEMOCRATS WIN ELECTION TO THE U.S. HOUSE OF REPRESENTATIVES

MAYBE WE SHOULD GO BACK TO THE 1980S...THAT WAS A TOUGH TIME FOR THE DEMOCRATIC PARTY.

AH, THE *REAGAN YEARS*. THE BERLIN WALL. THE AIR TRAFFIC CONTROLLERS. REAGANOMICS. SUNRISE IN AMERICA...

IRAN CONTRA...

THE ASSASSINATION ATTEMPT ON REGAN'S LIFE – IN 1981 – ONLY MADE HIM *MORE* POPULAR. HERE WAS AN OLD MAN WHO WAS *TOUGH* ENOUGH TO TAKE A BULLET AND SURVIVE.

SEEMED EVERYONE LOVED OUR COWBOY PRESIDENT.

WHEN REAGAN WAS IN OFFICE, NANCY PELOSI WAS AN ACTIVE MEMBER OF THE DEMOCRATIC NATIONAL COMMITTEE. IN 1984, SHE SERVED AS THE CHAIR OF THE DEMOCRATIC NATIONAL CONVENTION HELD IN SAN FRANCISCO.

IT WAS HER JOB TO FIGURE OUT A WAY FOR THE DEMOCRATIC PARTY TO REGAIN ITS FOOTING.

I'D LOVE TO SEE WHAT *THOSE* IDEAS WERE.

WHATEVER THEY WERE, THEY MUST HAVE MADE AN IMPACT. NANCY BECAME A RISING STAR IN THE DEMOCRATIC PARTY. CAMPAIGNING WAS IN HER *BLOOD*, PASSED ON FROM TOMMY THE ELDER, NO DOUBT. SHE WORKED HARD TO GET OTHER DEMOCRATS IN OFFICE.

IT WASN'T UNTIL 1987 THAT SOMEONE FINALLY CONVINCED NANCY THAT SHE SHOULD RUN FOR OFFICE *HERSELF*.

BEFORE SHE DIED IN EARLY 1987, SHE TOLD HER BROTHER-IN-LAW THAT NANCY SHOULD RUN FOR HER SEAT.

HER FRIEND, SALA BURTON, WAS A U.S. REPRESENTATIVE FROM SAN FRANCISCO. SHE WAS DYING FROM CANCER AND HAD ALREADY DECIDED NOT TO RUN FOR RE-ELECTION IN 1988.

THAT DECISION BY SALA BURTON WOULD EVENTUALLY CHANGE U.S. HISTORY.

IN 1987, THEN, NANCY PELOSI RAN HER FIRST CAMPAIGN FOR HERSELF, FIGHTING TO BECOME THE U.S. REPRESENTATIVE FROM THE 5TH CONGRESSIONAL DISTRICT OF CALIFORNIA.

HOW STRONG ARE WE IN THE FILMORE DISTRICT?

WE'RE LOOKING GOOD.

BRITT'S PRETTY STRONG EVERYWHERE, TOO, THOUGH.

BRITT WAS *HARRY BRITT*, NANCY'S OPPONENT IN THAT FIRST RACE. HE WAS A DEMOCRAT *AND* A HOMOSEXUAL.

WOW. AND HE LOST THAT RACE HOW?

THE MOOD WAS TENSE THAT NIGHT AT PELOSI CAMPAIGN HEADQUARTERS.

NANCY PELOSI: A VOICE THAT WILL BE HEARD

THAT SLOGAN CERTAINLY TURNED OUT TO BE PROPHETIC. YOU CAN'T *NOT* HEAR THAT VOICE THESE DAYS.

NANCY PELOSI

NANCY WAS 46 WHEN SHE RAN THAT FIRST SUCCESSFUL CAMPAIGN, BEATING BRITT BY ABOUT 2,000 VOTES IN THE DEMOCRATIC PRIMARY.

THIS BEING SAN FRANCISCO, WINNING THE DEMOCRATIC PRIMARY WAS AS GOOD AS WINNING THAT CONGRESSIONAL SEAT. IN JUNE OF 1987, PELOSI EASILY BEAT REPUBLICAN CANDIDATE HARRIETT ROSS – GETTING 62 PERCENT OF THE VOTE – TO HEAD OFF TO THE HOUSE OF REPRESENTATIVES FOR THE FIRST TIME.

LIKE EVERY OTHER SANE PERSON IN THIS COUNTRY, PELOSI WAS HORRIFIED AT THE BUSH ADMINISTRATION'S RESPONSE TO HURRICANE KATRINA. SHE WAS VOCAL WITH HER CRITICISMS OF FEMA.

THAT'S THE PROBLEM. IT'S EASY TO CRITICIZE. IT'S HARD TO ACTUALLY DO SOMETHING.

AS MINORITY LEADER, NANCY CONTINUED TO FIGHT FOR HER PERSONAL CAUSES: PROMOTING ENERGY INDEPENDENCE AND ALTERNATIVE FUELS, REFORMING HEALTH INSURANCE AND HEALTH CARE, AND RAISING THE MINIMUM WAGE.

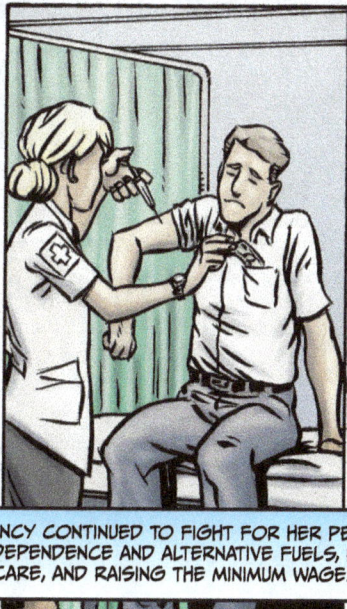

LIBERAL, LIBERAL, LIBERAL...CHECK.

I DID **NOT** HAVE SEXUAL RELATIONS WITH THAT WOMAN.

OOPS, DID I SAY "NOT."

EVERYONE IN POLITICS IS **HUMAN**, YOU KNOW. WE ALL DO THINGS THAT UPSET OTHERS, EVEN OUR SUPPORTERS AT TIMES. WE ALL MAKE MISTAKES. LORD KNOWS I MADE A FEW ERRORS IN THE PAST.

WHEN I PARDONED NIXON, A LOT OF PEOPLE WANTED TO TAR AND FEATHER ME. OTHERS THOUGHT IT WAS THE **WISE** THING TO DO.

IT'S PERFECTLY NATURAL, THEN, FOR A POLITICIAN TO HAVE FOLKS WHO ABSOLUTELY **HATE** HER.

IT'S ALL PART OF OUR POLITICAL PROCESS.

COVER THE CONTROVERSY.

RON SAYS "HI." AND HE'S WAITING FOR HIS OWN BOOK.

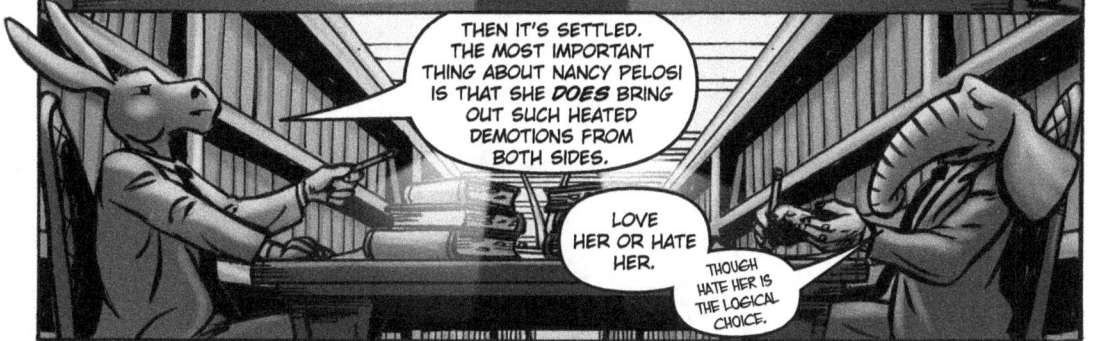

BLUEWATER COMICS

★ FEMALE ★ FORCE ★

Nancy Pelosi

Dan Rafter — Writer

Oski Yañez — Art

Kirsty Swan — Colorist

Wilson Ramos Jr. — Letterer

Darren G. Davis — Graphics

Darren G. Davis
Publisher

Jason Schultz
Vice President

Lisa K. Brause
Entertainment Manager

Crystal VanDiver
Director

Lisa Battan
Marketing Director

Janda Tithia
Coordinator

Scott Davis
Media Manager

Kim Sherman
Marketing Director

Vonnie Harris
New Business

Adam Ellis
Coordinator

Cover: Jim McDermott

Patrick Foster
Logo Design

Adam Ellis
Production

BLUEWATER COMICS

www.bluewaterprod.com

www.ingramcontent.com/pod-product-compliance
Lightning Source LLC
Chambersburg PA
CBHW081236020426
42331CB00012B/3195